Livonia Public Library
CIVIC CENTER #32
32777 Five Mile Road
Livonia, Michigan 48154
734.466.2491

CRAFTING WITH NATURE
SEED CRAFTS

BY BETSY RATHBURN

Express!

BELLWETHER MEDIA • MINNEAPOLIS, MN

Imagination comes alive in **Express!** Transform the everyday into the fresh and new, discover ways to stir up flavor and excitement, and experiment with new ideas and materials. Express! makerspace books: where your next creative adventure begins!

This edition first published in 2020 by Bellwether Media, Inc.

No part of this publication may be reproduced in whole or in part without written permission of the publisher. For information regarding permission, write to Bellwether Media, Inc., Attention: Permissions Department, 6012 Blue Circle Drive, Minnetonka, MN 55343.

Library of Congress Cataloging-in-Publication Data

Names: Rathburn, Betsy, author.
LC record for Seed Crafts available at https://lccn.loc.gov/2019035144

Text copyright © 2020 by Bellwether Media, Inc. BLASTOFF! READERS and associated logos are trademarks and/or registered trademarks of Bellwether Media, Inc.

Editor: Rebecca Sabelko   Designer: Andrea Schneider

Printed in the United States of America, North Mankato, MN.

Table of Contents

Time to Craft!	4
Pine Cone Roses	6
Pine Cone Succulent Garden	8
Pine Cone Bird Feeder	10
Seed Sunset	12
Dandelion Seed Necklace	14
Walnut Shell Keepsake	16
Maple Seed Butterfly	18
Seed and Leaf Fairy	20
Glossary	22
To Learn More	23
Index	24

Time to Craft!

Time to explore nature! Go outside and gather seeds. Pine cones and acorns contain tiny seeds that grow into huge trees. Maple seeds are also common. Other seeds, like beans and nuts, are good for crafting, too. These are easy to find at grocery stores.

When you have gathered your materials, it is time to craft! You can make jewelry, decorations, and even animal feeders with seeds.

PINE CONES

Common Seeds in the United States

MAPLE

SUNFLOWER

DANDELION

Nature Safety

- ✖ Have an adult check the area for any dangerous plants, animals, or other materials.
- ✖ Do not collect nature items from national or state parks.
- ✖ Ask permission to take items from yards or other private property.
- ✖ Stay away from animal nests and homes.
- ✖ Only collect as many supplies as needed.

Pine Cone Roses

Roses grow around the world. Most are found in the **Northern Hemisphere**.

The most common garden roses come from just 10 **species**. These species were **crossbred** to make new types of roses. Today, **hybrid** tea roses are some of the most popular. They were crossbred from two types of roses!

Paint the pine cones red, pink, yellow, or any other color.

Paint the sticks green.

When the pine cones and sticks are dry, glue one pine cone to the end of each stick.

materials

5 to 10 long sticks about 6 to 12 inches (15 to 30 centimeters) long

paintbrushes

several colors of paint, including green

scissors

5 to 10 pine cones

SWEET SMELLING ROSE

Cabbage roses are large roses with many petals. They were first bred between the years 1600 and 1800. They are often used to make perfume!

CABBAGE ROSES

4 Using the pencil, trace leaf shapes onto the construction paper. Cut out the leaves and glue them to the sticks.

5 Continue making as many roses as you want. Place the completed roses into the jar or other container!

hot glue gun

hot glue sticks

small jar or other container

pencil

green construction paper

Pine Cone Succulent Garden

Succulents are plants that grow in dry deserts. They store water in thick leaves or stems. Like other plants, succulents have **stomata**. These parts take in gases and let out water.

Unlike most plants, succulent stomata stay closed during the day. This stops the plants from drying out in the hot sun. Instead, succulent stomata open at night!

STRING OF PEARLS

The string of pearls is a popular type of succulent. This plant looks like a long, beaded necklace!

STRING OF PEARLS

materials

5 to 10 pine cones of different sizes

scissors

several colors of paint, including green

paintbrushes

moss, pebbles, or other filler

a wide, shallow pot or other container

1

Using scissors, carefully cut the pine cones into different sizes.

2

Paint each pine cone piece a different color. They will look like succulents.

3 Fill the pot with moss, pebbles, or other filler material.

4 Place the pine cone halves into the pot with the cut ends facing down. Now you have your own succulent garden!

CRAFT TiP

Try adding details to make your pine cones look like real succulents. Use different colors for more variety!

Pine Cone Bird Feeder

1

Bird-watching is an activity that many people enjoy. **Binoculars** help people spot birds of all kinds. Bird feeders help draw these birds into backyards and nature areas.

In the United States, some of the most common backyard birds are blue jays, robins, and crows. These birds like to eat sunflower seeds, peanuts, corn kernels, and many other seeds and nuts!

Tie one end of the string around the pine cone, leaving at least 12 inches (30 centimeters) of string at the end.

materials

1 large pine cone

peanut or other nut butter

long piece of string at least 24 inches (61 centimeters) long

sunflower seeds, dried corn kernels, and any other seeds

spoon

small plate

2

Using the spoon, cover the pine cone in a thick layer of peanut or other nut butter.

3

Pour the seeds onto the plate and roll the pine cone in them until it is covered in seeds.

SEEdS iN SPACE

Sunflower seeds have been grown in space! Astronaut Don Pettit grew sunflowers from seeds aboard the International Space Station.

4 Tie the bird feeder to a low tree branch. Watch birds come to eat!

Seed Sunset

Sunsets are some of the most beautiful sights on Earth. Their colors are caused by **Rayleigh scattering**. Sunlight scatters when it travels through gases, such as those in Earth's **atmosphere**.

Rayleigh scattering makes the sky look blue during the day. But at sunset, sunlight must travel through a thicker atmosphere. Most blue light scatters. It makes the sky look red!

BLACK SKY

If there were no Rayleigh scattering, Earth's sky would look black!

1

Use the pencil to draw a beach sunset scene on the cardboard or wood. Include the ground, water, a palm tree, and the sun.

2

Glue the dried black beans to the cardboard to fill in the palm tree's trunk and leaves. It will look like the tree is in shadow.

3

Glue the sunflower seeds to the cardboard to fill in the water. Glue them in different directions to look like waves!

materials

pencil

sturdy piece of cardboard or wood

glue

dried kidney beans

dried black beans

dried pinto beans

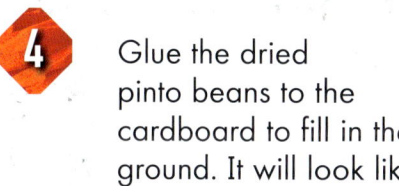
dried sunflower seeds

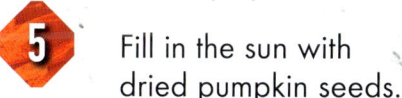
dried pumpkin seeds

dried corn kernels

4 Glue the dried pinto beans to the cardboard to fill in the ground. It will look like sand or grass.

5 Fill in the sun with dried pumpkin seeds.

6 Use dried kidney beans and dried corn kernels to create the sun's rays. When the glue is dry, find a place to display your seed art!

CRAFT TIP
Some seeds are not easy to find in nature. Buy beans and nuts at the grocery store to complete this craft!

Dandelion Seed Necklace

Dandelions are plants that grow throughout North America and Europe. They are famous for their yellow petals and thick stems.

As dandelions grow, their petals are replaced with wispy white seeds. They form a round shape called a blowball. Many people wish on dandelion blowballs. They blow the seeds away so more dandelions can grow!

More Than Weeds

Dandelion stems contain a liquid that is sometimes used to make rubber!

materials

at least 1 dandelion seed

open necklace pendant frame

Mod Podge® Dimensional Magic

string or cord about 20 inches (51 centimeters) long

clear packing tape

14

1

Set the pendant frame facedown on top of the packing tape. Press the frame firmly in place.

2 Pour the Mod Podge® Dimensional Magic into the frame until it is about half full. Let it dry until tacky.

3

Once the Mod Podge® is tacky, place the dandelion seeds on top of it.

4 Fill the rest of the frame with Mod Podge®. Let it dry for 3 days.

5 When the Mod Podge® is dry, carefully peel the frame away from the tape. The dandelion seeds should be visible through the pendant.

6 Thread the string or cord through the pendant's loop. Tie the ends into a knot. Now you have a dandelion necklace!

Walnut Shell Keepsake

Some common nuts are really seeds! Walnuts are one example. These nuts taste good, but they are not easy to get to. They are protected by shells.

Walnut shells grow in **husks** on walnut trees. The husks drop the shells to the ground. Animals or wind carry the shells away. If they are buried, a new walnut tree may grow!

Carefully glue the wooden bead to the inside of one end of the walnut shell. This will become an animal head.

Use the permanent marker to draw a face on the bead. Try making the face look asleep!

materials

half of a large walnut shell

hot glue gun

permanent marker

hot glue sticks

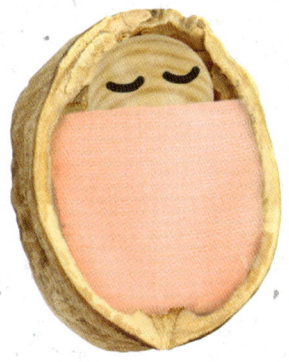

THAT'S NUTS!
Walnut husks can be used to make ink. Artists Vincent van Gogh and Rembrandt used walnut ink to write and sketch!

Carefully glue the fabric piece around the inside edges of the walnut shell, covering the bottom half of the bead. Trim away extra fabric if needed.

 Glue the ears to the top of the bead. Glue the hands to the top of the construction paper. Your sleepy keepsake is complete!

Draw hand and ear shapes on the construction paper and cut out.

construction paper

large wooden bead

scissors

pencil

small piece of fabric

maple seed Butterfly

There are more than 20,000 different butterfly species. Some live in one place their whole lives. But many butterfly species **migrate**.

Every spring, monarch butterflies migrate from Mexico to Canada. It takes many **generations** to complete the journey. Butterflies that reach Canada are the great-great grandchildren of those that left Mexico!

milkweed meals

Monarch butterflies begin as caterpillars. Their eggs hatch on milkweed plants. They eat as much milkweed as they can before turning into butterflies!

materials

- 90 to 100 maple seeds
- three different colors of paint
- paintbrushes
- thick piece of regular-sized paper
- glue
- pencil

Use the paintbrushes to paint the maple seeds. Paint around 40 of the first color, 30 of the second color, and 20 of the third color.

Layer maple seeds of the second color on top of the first row. Glue in place.

While the painted maple seeds dry, use the pencil to draw a butterfly shape onto the paper.

Layer maple seeds of the third color on top of the second row. Glue in place.

Add a layer of unpainted maple seeds to the center of the butterfly to make the body. Now you have a colorful maple seed butterfly!

Following the lines of the butterfly drawing, glue maple seeds of the first color around the edges of the wings.

Seed and Leaf Fairy

Fairies are **legendary** creatures that are common in children's stories. Many people once believed they were real. They were said to be magical creatures that looked like tiny humans.

In the early 1900s, the Cottingley Fairies became famous. A photo showed fairies dancing near a young woman. But the photo was a **hoax**. The fairies were made of paper cutouts!

1

Glue the small wooden ball to the flat bottom of the pine cone. This is the fairy's head.

2
Cut the construction paper into 10 to 20 thin strips, each about 6 inches (15 centimeters) long.

3
For each strip, fold a small section backwards. Then, fold the first section forward. Continue until each strip is folded end to end like a fan.

materials

one pine cone

small, wooden ball or bead

scissors

two large leaves

acorn top

4

Glue one end of each construction paper strip around the inside of the acorn top, leaving one side empty. This is the fairy's hair.

 5

Glue one end of the string to the inside of the acorn top. Make a loop across the outside, then glue the other end into the other side of the acorn top.

 6

Glue the acorn top to the top of the round ball. The part of the ball not covered by hair will be the fairy's face.

ANOTHER HOAX
Photo hoaxes were common before the Cottingley Fairies photo. In the 1800s, William H. Mumler created photos that were said to show ghosts!

7 Glue the two leaves to the back of the pine cone to make the fairy's wings. Now your fairy is complete!

piece of string about 6 inches (15 centimeters) long

hot glue gun

hot glue sticks

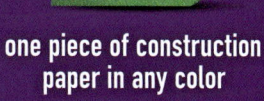
one piece of construction paper in any color

Glossary

atmosphere—the mix of gases that surrounds a planet or other body

binoculars—tools used to view faraway objects up close

crossbred—bred one type of plant with another type of plant to make a new plant

generations—groups of living things that came from older groups of the same living things

hoax—an act meant to trick other people

husks—the outer coverings of seeds and fruits

hybrid—made by combining two different types of something

legendary—well known or famous

migrate—to move from one place to another, often with the seasons

Northern Hemisphere—the part of the earth that is north of the equator

Rayleigh scattering—a process in which light scatters and bends when it hits tiny objects, causing different colors

species—different types of plants, animals, and other living things

stomata—small openings in plants that take in gases and let out water

to learn more

AT THE LIBRARY

Beaton, Clare. *Read, Make, & Create: The Nature Craft Book*. Waterstown, Mass.: Charlesbridge, 2019.

Golkar, Golriz. *Learn About Seeds*. Mankato, Minn.: Child's World, 2019.

Stewart, Melissa. *A Seed is the Start*. Washington, D.C.: National Geographic, 2018.

ON THE WEB

FACTSURFER

Factsurfer.com gives you a safe, fun way to find more information.

1. Go to www.factsurfer.com.

2. Enter "seed crafts" into the search box and click.

3. Select your book cover to see a list of related web sites.

index

beans, 4, 13
birds, 10
common seeds, 5
Cottingley Fairies, 20, 21
craft tips, 9, 13
dandelion seed necklace, 14-15
dandelions, 14
hoax, 20, 21
maple seed butterfly, 18-19
monarch butterflies, 18
nature safety, 5
nuts, 4, 10, 13, 16
pine cone bird feeder, 10-11
pine cone roses, 6-7
pine cone succulent garden, 8-9
Rayleigh scattering, 12
roses, 6, 7
seed and leaf fairy, 20-21
seed sunset, 12-13
succulents, 8, 9
sunflower seeds, 10, 11
walnut shell keepsake, 16-17
walnuts, 16, 17

The images in this book are reproduced through the courtesy of: Andrea Schneider/ Bellwether Media, front cover, pp. 2, 5-21 (all crafts); Scott Sanders, p. 4 (acorns); nuchstockphoto, p. 4 (inset); Kathy Clark, p. 5 (maple seeds); thewet nonthachai, p. 5 (sunflower seeds); Bess Hamitii, p. 5 (dandelion seeds); Jekatarinka, p. 7 (cabbage roses); kura_diamond, p. 9 (string of pearls).